MIDLIFE CRASH

HOW I LEARNED TO COPE WITH CRISIS

GALE DURAN

Fillinger – Grau

HIGH BRIDGE BOOKS
HOUSTON

Dedication

I dedicate this book to my entire family as they walked alongside me during my grieving years with the loss of my husband. A very special dedication to my two daughters who were constantly there for me, offering comfort and love over all these years.

To; Stevie Copp Brown
1967 Class of Danbury

From: Gale Fellinger-Brau
Duran

6-3-2022

Contents

Introduction

It is my hope that anyone reading this book will realize "God has a purpose and a plan for your life, and it is for *good!*" (Jer. 29:11).

At age 44, my husband died unexpectedly of a massive heart attack. Of course, I was in shock. However, God opened doors to give me hope and a new life. As Psalm 23 tells us:

> Even though I walk through the valley of the
>   shadow of death, I will fear no evil,
> for you are with me; your rod and your staff,
>   they comfort me. (Ps. 23:4 ESV)

1

A New Baby Sister

It was late in the day on September 3, 1949, when Lee felt a slight contraction in her stomach. This was her fourth child, so the contraction was not a surprise.

Lee continued to pick peaches, as it was her job in the summer. She and her husband, Howard, had an orchard with apples and peaches. The crop this year was a "bumper" producing hundreds of bushels of the Red Haven variety. As she continued to pick the peaches, the contractions got stronger and stronger. She decided to call Howard and inform him of the upcoming trip to the hospital to deliver their fourth child.

She left the orchard, walked toward the house, and found Howard in the backyard unloading peaches from a wagon. She sauntered up to the wagon and took a hold of his strong hand, looking into his dark brown eyes. Somehow he read her eyes, telling him that she was in labor and they needed to get to the hospital ASAP. He quickly finished placing the last basket of peaches onto the wagon, and they hurried into the house to get their suitcase. They quickly gathered the other three children and got them into the car. The grandparents lived close by, so they would drop them off and head to the local hospital. All three children were very excited to welcome their new brother or sister when the baby was brought home. Home was a small city located on the shores of Lake Erie in Northern Ohio. The family had lived here for several years with the other three children—a boy and two girls who had entered the world at this same local hospital. The little city was known as a vacation land for hundreds of people. The city offered several excellent beaches and state parks packed with families enjoying the great outdoors. This was *home* for this little family.

At the hospital, Howard got Lee admitted to the labor and delivery unit where her family physician cared for her. After the doctor evaluated her labor progress, he asked Howard to leave and wait out in the visitor's lounge. This was a very tense moment for the couple, as Lee was a very small woman and her other babies were delivered under much duress. Howard waited in suspense as the hours ticked slowly by, minute by minute, hour by hour.

After three hours, the doctor came out to get Howard and announced that he was the proud father of a little red-headed girl.

Howard was allowed to go to the room where Lee was resting in her bed. The baby was tucked away in the nursery fast asleep while the proud daddy looked on at his amazing baby girl. Yes, she did have red hair and beautiful blue eyes like her mommy. He was very excited as well as surprised to find out it was a little girl, as in 1949, there were no sonograms to inform you before the baby arrived. Howard was walking on water and so happy to rejoice with Lee about their new daughter! After several hours, Howard left to pick up the other children from their grandparents' home and deliver the good news about their new baby sister!

After arriving at home with the children, Howard told them about their new baby sister and that she would be coming home in a week or two. The kids were so very excited to hear about their new sister and how they would be able to hold her and feed her the bottle of formula. They giggled and laughed, and then Howard put them to bed and kissed them. They said their prayers together before they fell asleep, dreaming about their new baby sister.

In the quiet, dark hospital room, Lee was almost asleep and praising her Lord and Savior for the amazing, healthy baby girl soon to be in her arms. She was remembering her loving husband and the three other children God had placed in her life. Just praise, praise, praise was all she could think about. From now on, it would be their little family in their tiny rented house with the full orchard to care for.

After a few minutes, she slipped off to sleep and dreamed about the new baby girl that she would soon hold in her arms. What a wonderful day this had been, and she was so happy she could hardly hold all the joy inside her tired body; however, she went into a deep sleep for the rest of the night,

Early the next morning, the nurse brought the sweet baby girl into Lee's room and placed the tiny child into her arms. The nurse brought in a bottle of warm milk so Lee could feed the baby and enjoy her soft, little body held close against hers.

She looked deep into the little girl's eyes and saw a bright twinkle that she had not noticed in the other children's eyes! How could that be? What did the twinkle indicate about the baby? Would she be a teacher? A chemist? A doctor? A missionary? A nurse? Just what was the little twinkle in that baby's eyes? She would have to wait a long, long time to find out just what God had in store for this little child with the red hair and deep blue eyes. Lee had a deep abiding faith in Jesus Christ, and she was absolutely sure that God had gifted her little girl with a joyful heart!

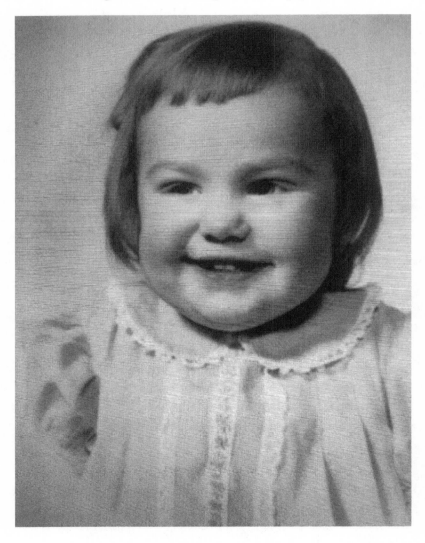

Time marched on and it was finally time for Howard to

pick Lee up from the hospital and take her and the baby home. The drive home was short. As they pulled into the driveway, the other three children rushed out. They couldn't wait to meet their new baby sister. They all went into the house and settled down in the living room, which was just what the new baby needed. Lee and the baby were very tired, and the entire family took a short nap before the afternoon was gone and night settled over the little house on the shores of Lake Erie.

2

What to Name the New Baby?

It was a very exciting September, and the name recorded on the birth certificate was Gale Corinne. They explained to the rest of the family that the name was chosen based on the popular television show called the "Gale Storm Show," which Howard and Lee had watched over the years. They selected the middle name Corinne after her paternal grandmother. This was an excellent choice because as the child grew up, she was very close to her grandmother.

When Gale was six weeks old, they selected their all-time best friends to be the godparents. Pauline and Harold were God-loving friends who lived close to the family. They contacted the pastor at their local church and selected the date for the baptism. The couple was just delighted to be chosen as godparents, and they started praying for the baby at once.

The date was set, and the little church was packed on that Sunday morning. All the immediate family and friends attended to witness the baptism of the baby girl Howard and Lee brought before the Lord to be baptized into the kingdom of God. The pastor asked the parents and godparents to place the Word of God into the child's hands and to walk alongside her throughout her life, guiding her into accepting Jesus Christ as her Savior and Lord. Both couples agreed to promise to teach the child about God and His love.

The day ended and the family gathered in the little rent house to celebrate with joy and happiness. That little girl, Gale Corrine, was me.

> *Raise up a child in the way he should go and when he is old, he will not depart from it.*
> *—Proverbs 22:6*

As time passed, I was taken to church and was taught how to pray with all my heart. I learned how to sing in the junior choir and loved attending Sunday School. My brother and two sisters and I attended church every Sunday. Our grandparents attended the same worship service, so the entire family sang, prayed, and learned about Jesus together every single week.

As the years went swiftly by, I decided to enter the study of Catechism, a summary of the Christian principles in the form of questions and answers. Each Saturday morning for two years, I attended with my friends to learn and understand the Christian faith. We studied the Lord's prayer, the Ten Commandments, and the Apostles Creed so I could understand what the Christian faith was all about.

Later I was asked to join the church as a believer and attend the services as a member. Wow, this was a formal, serious decision. We had to come before the entire congregation and be questioned about our belief in God. The entire class faced the people in their seats and answered the questions one by one. And then we were asked to join the church and be active members serving the church as well as the community. We all agreed to join the church and be-come followers of Christ.

At the same time, my family moved from the little rented house to a huge farmhouse that our grandparents lived in. Because of grandpa's failing health, they moved into a smaller home and my entire family moved into the homestead. This was an amazing time in my life, as the house was an old boarding home and had two kitchens and six bedrooms. Each child had their own bedroom, and the farm had several barns filled with cattle and pigs. It was a dream come true for me. The future held many fun adven-tures for me and my entire family over the coming years. Holidays were filled with love, laughter, and family—abundance and joy abounded!

3

A Horse for Me

Now that the entire family had moved into the new home, each child had their own bedroom and acres and acres of farmland to discover. Soon our grandmother opened a covered wagon fruit stand, which offered all vacationers fresh peaches, sweet corn, green beans, and crisp apples in season. Hundreds of vacationers from the Cleveland suburbs stopped at the Old Covered Wagon market located in our front yard.

My grandmother opened the stand every morning and offered fresh local honey to all the guests. Soon there was a huge garden with fresh tomatoes and other vegetables to offer travelers. It was always fun to be around family as we worked together to make the stand a huge success. We spent many summers around the covered wagon, greeting strangers seeking out fresh produce to take back to their homes to enjoy with their meals.

One Father's Day in June, a tragedy occurred. As my loving grandfather was sitting under the large maple tree in the front yard, he had a major stroke. Following this medical emergency, we placed a hospital bed in the second living room and my grandmother cared for him over the next year. After his stroke, he was speechless and could only mumble incoherently. It was magical how my grand-mother could decipher his mumbles and get him a bedpan or a drink. Over that year, I witnessed my grandmother's love for my suffering grandfather. What a witness of love and devotion as well as commitment

They had been married for many years. My grandfa-ther was hired by the railroad back in the early 1900s, and their family moved many times over the years. They lived in Massachusetts. Vermont, Virginia, and several other states. My grandmother was a very faithful, committed Christian throughout her entire life. She married my grand-father at a young age and stayed by his side, encouraging him over 50 years before his stroke took his life.

My family eventually buried my grandfather and con-tinued our lives on the farm. After the funeral, my father and big brother assumed the job of milking the cows and feeding the pigs for market as the time rolled on without my grandfather. Life on the farm was amazing — baby kit-tens, puppies, lambs, baby pigs, and baby calves all the time, fun, fun, fun.

My maternal grandfather loved horses and so did I. When I turned nine years old, I begged my dad to get me a horse. After many months of my begging, whining, and crying, he said, "Let's get Gale a horse." Now remember, we lived on a farm and milked over 20 cows every single day and money was tight. We were happy as a family, but sometimes we were forced to charge the groceries at the lo-cal store and pay at the end of the month when we sold a cow. So purchasing a horse was a huge decision, and ex-pensive. My dad sold an old corn grinder for $100.00. Now, you may wonder what kind of a horse you can buy for that amount of money. Well, we looked in the local newspaper and there he was—one large horse for sale: $100.00, saddle and bridle included. So my dad, brother, and grandfather went to look at the horse, and later that day, around the corner came our 1949 red Studebaker pickup truck with a large white horse riding on the back.

That was the start of a 15-year friendship with that wonderful, large white horse. Whenever I had a good day or bad day, that horse was always there for me through thick and thin, rain, sleet, or snow. I joined the local 4-H club and won Champion Horsemanship and Showmanship for two years. The two of us were seen in the local neighborhood riding down lanes and visiting neighbors day in and day out.

A girl in my neighborhood had used her aunt's horse, and we went riding together over hill and dale. Many times, I rode her horse in a local rodeo on Sunday afternoons, enjoying contests and friends. Trail rides and campouts with other horse friends led to many happy times over many years and friendships that would last a lifetime.

4

The Nail and the Wedding

Time flew by so quickly. I had entered school and was riding my horse all over the county. I took good care of my horse every single day. I brushed his coat, protected him with fly spray, and always fed him fresh, clean oats. Together we were a good team!

Now, one day I did not feed the horse before the school bus picked me up. So my dad said, "No worries, I will see that your horse gets fed and watered right away." When Dad stepped down from the milk house onto the barn floor, what a shock! As the heavy weight of a six-foot man dropped to the floor, pain shot through his foot! Whoa, what just happened? It felt like a knife went into his foot and the pain seared through his entire leg and into his back. As he looked down, he saw a board with a very sharp nail sticking out of it. He had stepped down on the nail with the full force of his weight.

He quickly pulled the board down so that the nail would come out of his foot, but the pain remained! Then he hobbled quickly back to the house, where my mom was doing dishes in the kitchen. She was very shocked as he limped into the house with blood all over his shoe. They took his shoe off and she rinsed his foot with warm, soapy water, but to no avail. The puncture wound was very serious and required immediate medical attention.

Mom loaded Dad into the car, and they raced to the local hospital emergency room. Once at the hospital, Howard was loaded into a wheelchair and pushed into the emergency room where a doctor could treat his wound. First, the doctor flushed out the dried blood and dirt. Then they took several X-rays of the wound to evaluate the damage.

The x-rays showed several chipped bones in his foot that the nail had pierced through. The doctors admitted him to the hospital for intravenous antibiotic treatments. Mom returned home and continued doing the chores on the farm with the help of her oldest son. It was a long night for Mom, as she was very concerned about Dad's health and how long he would have to stay in the hospital.

The very next day, she returned to the hospital for an update on Dad's condition. The report was not good. The doctor said there was an infection in the bone called osteomyelitis. The infection was causing inflammation in the bone and spreading to the rest of his body. The doctor recommended taking off his leg to save his life. Mom did not agree but asked if there was another choice. The doctor mentioned a new experimental drug just out on the market and asked Mom if they wanted to try it. Mom prayed and decided to take the chance and try the new drug. The treatment was started right away.

Progress was evaluated five days later, and it was outstanding! Dad's temperature had dropped several points and the swelling in his leg had gone down dramatically. Dad didn't need his leg removed, and all was looking like good news.

One thing changed throughout this time. As I visited

my dad, I began spending a lot of time with my dad's room-mate—the young man in the first bed. After several days, I was spending more time with him than with my dad.

That is how it all began. I started dating this young man when they both got out of the hospital. We all became good friends, but this young man was very much in love with me and I was only 16. My parents were concerned about this new romance and thought I was much too young to be involved in a serious relationship.

As time went on, the young man joined the National Guard and was transferred to basic training in Maryland for six months. Over this period, I received letters from my young friend, as he was stationed in Maryland at the Fort Mead army base. One letter stated that he was coming home on leave for the weekend and wanted me to be his date at a friend's wedding.

My mother and father were very concerned about the blossoming relationship. However, they approved of the young man because he was raised by a local Christian farm couple. They gave me permission to go on the date with the new young soldier. The curfew was rigid, and I needed to be home by midnight after the wedding and reception were over.

The wedding was beautiful, with the groom and bride promising to be committed until death. Their love was very obvious. The couple would work a local farm together raising cattle and making a loving home for the future children to make their family complete. After the reception ended, the young man delivered me back home before midnight. Of course, my mom and dad were watching for our arrival and blinked the porch light several times to indicate it was time to come into the house.

After several years of dating and family times, the young man proposed to me on Christmas Eve with a diamond engagement ring. My answer was yes and, 10 months later we were married in my little church. The reception was held in the local armory, where my new husband had been serving in the local National Guard. The band was comprised of local friends and the place was packed with friends and family sliding over the dance floor and celebrating the new married couples' lives together.

After the wedding, we went on a honeymoon to Niagara Falls and Canada. We drove up through Canada and then back down through New York City. What an amazing start to our lives together. We even went through the Sault Saint Marie Locks in Michigan while touring in a horse-drawn carriage.

Upon returning home, we rented an apartment, and my new husband went back to full-time employment—

working three different shifts and determined to make a wonderful, stable living for us. We were very much in love and committed to staying married until death do us part. We were filled with joy and happiness. We were deeply committed Christians, being raised in farm-family homes and brought up in the Lutheran faith.

Both of us had strong prayer lives and prayed together daily. We prayed about starting a family and how we would raise our children. Be sure to pray for God's guidance in your life. Wait, Pray, Listen, and know what God wants you to do with your life. Don't make mistakes in this area. All of us need God's guidance, and we need to run to Him with our requests and then listen to His voice.

5

Country Living

Two years later, we were blessed with a precious little daughter and moved into a farmhouse in the country. Of course, I brought my horse along to the farm and rode him while carrying my new baby. As the months rolled on, we enjoyed our new daughter, and she made the entire family giggle with glee. She was a happy baby, and we had her baptized in our local church, promising to bring her up in the Christian faith. "Raise up a child in the way he should go; and when she is old, she will not depart from it." (Prov. 22:6)

I asked my sister and brother-in-law to become faithful godparents to this lovely little girl. Over the years, they placed the Bible into her hands and took her to Sunday School to learn about God's love for her. They were consistent in their promise for over 50 years in our daughter's life. They prayed for her and reminded her of her commitment to her Christian values and to listen to God's voice in her choices.

Two years later, we were blessed with yet another precious daughter, and that made our family complete. This little girl was a quiet baby and made everyone smile when they looked into her little blue eyes. At the first doctor's visit, he noticed the baby's legs were very crooked, so she was fitted with a brace to wear over the next year. With these corrective shoes, her legs would be straightened out and in her adult life, she became an amazing dancer.

This child was also baptized into the family of God and had godparents promise to love and guide her in the way of the Christian faith, with prayers and love. As this little girl grew, the Bible promised her that "God has a plan and a purpose in your life" (Jer. 29:11). Her godparents guided her and prayed for her over her youth, and God heard the prayers and showed her what path to take during her lifetime. She was blessed. She studied dance in her college career.

Everything seemed to be going along smoothly, and then came the riots on the Ohio State and Kent State campuses. My husband was called away by the National Guard to be present in case of violence. After several weeks, he returned home just to be sent to summer camp for two weeks for training.

At this time, we put the farmhouse up for sale and moved into a small home inside the city limits. The neighbors were close by, and I got hired with Ohio State Co-Operative Service, serving as a 4-H youth director in the county. This was an amazing job, as I always loved working with children and was in 4-H myself for over 10 years with my horse. The job was a dream come true. I would be working in the county where I grew up, and I knew all of the local schools. I knew many local people because I had been in the 4-H program for 10 years, and I knew how valuable the program was for our youth.

6

4-H Youth Program Assistant

I applied for the job with Ohio State, and the interview was scheduled. Afterward, the agent offered the position to me. Wow, unbelievable. I was now a youth assistant for the county 4-H program! My job included visiting schools in the county to enroll youth in the 4-H program offered through the university. The position also offered a boat ride to Kelleys Island in Lake Erie for a week-long camp with 200 children. The camp included singing, swimming, dancing, and, of course, campfire times. Our two daughters attend the camp, and as they grew older, they served as camp counselors in a leadership position.

One spectacular feature of the job included a county fair event, which included horse shows, carnival rides, and famous stage icons such as Brooks and Dunn playing their top hits. The fair also included camping and offered week-long events on stage as well as horse racing. The fair closed with a greased pig contest, allowing children to chase and capture their own little pig to take home.

The job also included working with older youth and training them for leadership positions as well as trips to tour the Ohio State campus. The older students were offered local job opportunities to further their own education.

Many youths went to the state capital to meet with the state representatives. Many applied for college scholarships and were awarded large sums of funding to further their education. Overall, the 4-H program offered a challenge to every child included in their local club events.

One part of my job with the University was to visit local schools and introduce the 4-H program to the area youth. There were over 200 programs to choose from. Some of the projects were computers, woodworking, veterinarian science, nutrition, fashion design, horsemanship, genealogy, and electricity programs.

Each member who joined pledged their head to clearer thinking, their heart to greater loyalty, their hands to larger service, and their health for better living — for their community, country, and their world. This pledge was adopted in 1927 and is still part of 4-H today!

I enjoyed my position with Ohio State University for 10 years. Then I was let go, and my time with the 4-H program was completed. Both daughters were now high school graduates and had entered college. Now what? What was the next chapter for my life at this point? Where would I go? What would I do? The next step looked like college at the age of 36! So I enrolled at Toledo University and started a new career! What would I be when I grew up?

7

College Bound

Over the past 23 years, life had been good—married, children, jobs, weddings, funerals, parties, birthday cele- brations, graduations, and much, much more. Parenting was an important job! Again, "Train up a child how they should go, and when they get old, they will not depart from it." Proverbs 22:6 is a promise from the Bible, and our chil- dren had been raised in the Christian faith.

Over the years, our home had been a haven for foster children who needed love and affection. This program proved to benefit both our family and the foster children. We housed over 10 children and babies. Many children who came to our home arrived with a garbage bag of belongings. This was a sad arrival; however, our family was full of love and Christian morals that we smothered the children with as we all sat down at the dinner table together, prayed, and ate our food together.

The children attended Sunday School and Vacation Bi- ble School with our daughters. Many of the children had been abused by their parents and told they were a waste of skin. Of course, this needed to be addressed, and our home was a place of unconditional love. The Bible tells us, "For God so loved the World, that he gave his only begotten son, that whoever believes in Him would be saved" (John 3:16). These foster children needed to be loved and taught the Word of God. Our family provided a safe haven for each and every child who came into our home! We were blessed by each child and enjoyed every minute of the time spent with our farm family.

Now with both daughters off to college and the foster children no longer in our home, it opened the door for me to attend college—a dream I always had since childhood. The university was an hour's drive from the little farm where she lived, and it was a challenge to drive, complete homework, and keep the household chores up to date. I was dedicated to the challenge. I drove back and forth to Toledo, attended classes, and did my homework while visiting the campus library. I enrolled in several different classes such as communications, sociology, and business courses. I spent time with my assigned academic advisor being counseled on which courses were best for me to take.

The advisor was a perfect match for me as a non-traditional student entering college at the age of 36! What would I be when I grew up? A teacher? A lawyer? A doctor? A dentist? A nurse? Just what would I be when I finished college? I attended all my classes, and when I completed the communications class, it all exploded! This is where I choose my major area of study. In third grade, my favorite teacher always said, "Gale always likes to talk, talk, talk." So this seemed like a good fit!

For the next three years, I attended college classes and completed all assignments. I made many friends and worked in the Dean's office to defray my expenses. I applied for a scholarship and was awarded funds from Clairol simply because I was *old*"! I joined a non-traditional student group, and it was wonderful for the older students to attend. Then I continued my studies in communications, I joined the Women in Communications organization. This group supported all my ideas for new career opportunities. I was invited to attend local programs that would enhance my future resume'.

Throughout these years, my marriage was under much stress, as my husband and I didn't spend much time together. He was working 14 days straight with one day off. This was a hard road to travel for us in addition to the stress we both faced in the commitment to completing our goals. We spent time together on the weekends, but that was rare and very far between. My college career was important, but my marriage was more important, and I was committed to making things work out.

Throughout our marriage, my husband was a heavy drinker and consumed all types of alcohol every day—so much that he would pass out and vomit. If things didn't change and his drinking didn't decrease, there would be very serious consequences.

At this time, his cholesterol was over 300. The doctors had warned him about his condition, but he continued to consume beer on a daily basis. I urged him to attend AA and get some help, but he resisted. He continued to work every single day and drank with gusto. I continued my studies, and the girls continued their college work with steadfast commitment.

One daughter was getting a nursing degree, with a specialization in heart transplant. She later moved to Texas and got a full-time position with Dallas Children's Hospital. At first, she was working in the heart transplant unit and was later promoted to the flight area. This unit had her transporting patients from car accidents in a life-flight pattern. After that, she moved into the recovery unit, so she could home after she got married.

My other daughter was majoring in dance and kinesiology. She was selected to join and perform with Up with People International. For the next year, my talented daughter danced and entertained all over the world with this group. She traveled to Australia and performed in large arenas.

She also performed in the famous Super Bowl Halftime show that year as the featured entertainment. This was an excellent opportunity in her life, and she gained experience from the travel and lived with several families over the years, giving her many opportunities to grow in her life through traveling to countries all over the world.

My older daughter, Teresa

My younger daughter, Tamara

8

Graduation

The day had arrived—the completion of my college career. Throughout the challenges and hurdles, I had taken my final exam and would be awarded my degree in communications. The stage was set, the invitations were sent out, and the ceremony was beginning. How exciting for my family, friends, and coworkers to attend the graduation ceremony and see this 40-year-old lady receive her diploma! I could hardly believe it was happening. The day I had dreamed about was finally here, and I was so excited I could hardly breathe.

The ceremony began with the processional of all the students filing into the auditorium to be seated in front of the audience. The hall was packed, and every seat was occupied. One by one, the names were called to go up on stage to be awarded their diplomas. Finally, I heard my name called and I walked onto the stage. I stopped at the microphone and presented my heartfelt appreciation to my parents, family, and friends.

While I was finishing my degree, I nominated my parents for the "Parents of the Year Award." At that moment, my parents were announced as recipients of the coveted award! What a spectacular moment in their lives to be given this honor! Unbelievable! My parents were asked to come up on stage to receive the award. The auditorium was filled with applause, and my parents were in total disbelief. What a thrill! Over all the years of hard, dedicated parenting, the time had come for them to be appreciated. They had raised me just like the Bible instructed, and now that I was old, I had not departed from that training and would now move forward. I let my light shine before others and give the glory to God my Father in Heaven (Matt. 5:16).

After the ceremony, everyone filed into the party room to celebrate with me on my outstanding accomplishment. There were many hugs and high fives during the party as well as rejoicing! Everyone enjoyed the food and drinks, and then came the awards to my family, friends, and teachers. I gave a very special award to my husband for being there for me while I completed my college degree. I also honored my teachers and the Dean for hiring me to work in her office to pay my expenses. Finally, I offered awards to all my friends, classmates, and those who encouraged me to complete my education.

Then came the moment to pack up, leave, and return home. The entire day was just a blur in my mind. I began to ask myself, did this event really happen or was it just a dream? I was so very happy that I felt like I was walking on air. What a day to remember forever and ever. My dream of a college education had come true, and I would start a new chapter in my life! The challenges and changes I'd face would take courage and strength as I leaned on the Lord and not my own understanding. I had been taught as a youth to be patient, loving, and filled with joy, hope, and courage—loving myself and others through Christ. I turned to prayer and praise to listen to the voice of God as I made many challenging changes in my midlife.

9

Crash

The very next day my husband and I had a tremendous decision to work through. I was being offered a new job teaching at South West Texas college. What would I do? How could I decide whether to move to Texas or stay in Ohio? The discussion was fueled by the impact of alcohol on my husband. He was definitely not interested in leaving his job and moving to Texas. What would we do? The drinking increased, and I got some counseling on making a decision. The counselor suggested that I take the teaching job and persuade my husband to move to Texas. Would my husband listen and support his wife's dreams? Time would tell. The days passed slowly on and on!

The time arrived, and my husband told me to move to Texas, get an apartment, and take the teaching job. He was not interested in leaving his job or stopping his consumption of alcohol, which had increased in leaps and bounds. He was now hiding bottles of booze behind his truck seat to keep me from knowing how much alcohol he was drinking every single day.

The day finally arrived, and my husband helped me load the rental truck I had secured. The car was attached to the trailer behind the truck. We kissed goodbye. I was off and away to Texas. Several days later, I arrived in the little town of San Marcos, Texas, where the college was located. When I pulled into the apartment complex, I had help unloading the furniture and prepared the kitchen with essential items. Then it was time for bed and to get some rest.

The trip had been long and tiresome, and I needed to catch up on my sleep. The apartment was so very quiet, and I was so lonely after living in a huge house with acreage, a barn, horses, dogs, goats, and pigs. The night dragged on, and the next day I would start my teaching career and work on earning my master's degree in communications.

The days sped past, and I taught during the day and attended graduate classes in the evening every day. I met a lot of new friends during classes as well as by attending the University women's club. They invited me to participate in 10K walks in several different cities. This was a fun activity, and I made many new friends.

Then I decided to find a church to worship my Lord and Savior. The church was near campus, and I was warmly welcomed into the congregation and the Sunday School class. I made many friends and created my own support system. The move was very upsetting, but I was sure that my husband would follow me to Texas in due time. I prayed for reconciliation for my marriage and for my husband to stop destroying his life with the abuse of alcohol.

Days, weeks, and months passed, and yet I remained alone in the apartment. I had chatted with my husband and daughters several times. It just broke my heart to miss the days and nights with them that we used to share over the last 24 years. Times were changing, and the future was in God's hands. I hesitated to move to Texas, but when I prayed, I heard the Holy Spirit whispering, "This is my

Father's World" and was covered with a strong peace that I was making the right choice to move. I was a strong prayer warrior.

When I was a child, I was taught to rush to Jesus to make my decisions, and my parents had raised me to continue to turn to Jesus. I remembered how my godparents had guided me to read the Scriptures and have a constant prayer life. I was experiencing a broken heart at the same time I was enjoying my new teaching position. I carried on with determination but cried myself to sleep every single night. I was very torn by my decision to move to Texas and yet repair my marriage, knowing I couldn't stop my husband's addiction to alcohol.

The next day before I woke up, the phone rang. I slid out of bed and answered the call. As I listened to the message, that was the moment my life *crashed*. After 26 years with my husband, moving into four different homes, raising two children, and getting into college, my life changed. This was the message:

"We are very sorry to inform you, but your husband has died of a massive heart attack." I could not believe the words that had just fallen on my ears. *What? This must be a mistake. What do you mean my husband is dead?* My entire world came crashing down all around me. I dropped the phone in shock and collapsed on my couch. What was happening? How could this be true? My husband was only 44, and the next day would have been his 45th birthday. He was much too young to die of a heart attack, right?

It was time to gather my thoughts and get to the airport. I needed to fly back to Ohio and face the fact that my husband was dead. Once I arrived at the Detroit Airport, my nephew picked me up and we sped back to my hometown.

At home, I was surrounded by my family, hugs, tears, and disbelief. Then it was time to visit the funeral home and create a loving memorial service for the family. Many family members were local; however, many of them were in several different cities throughout the state. It would take several days for them to travel to the funeral and attend the celebration of life.

Our daughters and I met at the funeral home to plan the memorial service. Many tasks needed to be completed before we could schedule the service to be held in four days. We had to gather all the materials, contact family and friends to inform them of the death, and reach out to ministers to perform the service. We received flowers, cards, food, and visits from friends from all parts of Ohio. What a shock, and what an amazing situation I was facing as my world *crashed* around me!

10

Celebration of Life

The day had arrived. The funeral home was packed with family, friends, and neighbors. Everyone offered their sympathy to me and the entire family. The pastor who had guided me as a youngster into my Christian faith and married me and my husband was in front of the room conducting the celebration of life. Wow, if any pastor knew our history, it was this man of God. He spoke with sincerity, poise, and love. He opened with an amazing prayer and welcomed all in attendance.

There was not an empty chair in the funeral home, as folks had come from many parts of the state and my husband dying young brought many together. We sang the "Old Rugged Cross." Then our youngest daughter who studied dance had prepared a special dance. She floated across the carpet and gave honor to her daddy as she stepped to the soft music. Over and over, she glided to the tune and said goodbye to him.

The other daughter wrote a poem to dedicate to her daddy. The poem was very powerful and filled with sincerity. She had a very difficult time speaking the poem because of her broken heart. Both girls loved their daddy and offered an amazing tribute to him!

The funeral ended, and then we dismissed to the local church for the bereavement banquet. The banquet hall was packed, and everyone enjoyed chatting, crying, and visiting over the delicious food. The day ended with much joy as well as sadness over the loss of our beloved husband, uncle, brother, father, son-in-law, and disciple of God. Life would be different from this moment on—empty but moving forward in faith, leaning on the Lord Jesus our Savior and Comforter. I remember the Bible verse saying, *"I can do all things through Christ, who strengths me" (Phil 4:13).*

*He promises to **never** leave us alone!* From that day on, I have lived a very different life leaning on the *Lord*!

11

Life After Death

Yes, after the funeral ceremony, life did go on and on! I was still in shock, and my husband's body was cremated as we had discussed beforehand. Several days passed and the ashes were delivered to me at home. Many friends and family dropped by for a visit, and other family members traveled back to their respective homes and cities. It all seemed like a nightmare, unbelievable!

When you lose a loved one, you may think the pain is too great to bear, but it is probably not. You may think you cannot get through another day, but most likely you can. You may tell yourself that you have reached your limit, but most of us have limits well beyond ourselves. You may think this is it! There is no way I can live like this any longer. But you can go on with God's help!

Reach out for help and support. Do not struggle alone! Do not remove the larva from the cocoon. Do not take away the irritating grain of sand from the oyster. If you do, you will never see the beautiful butterfly or the pearl glisten! In Psalm 103, David describes God as a tender father who loves his child with a special kind of love, lovingkindness. This love conveys the image of bending a knee to help someone in need.

After many months, still in shock, I returned to Texas and resumed my job teaching at the university. My church family surrounded me with prayers and love. I sought out every grief group in the local area I could find and shared my broken heart with others. This was a very important part of my healing, as I had left my family and friends back in Ohio. I made a concerted effort to cry and grieve over the loss of my husband in every group I attended. I knew my tears were really liquid love, and it helped me heal.

Back on the college campus, I resumed my teaching commitment as well as my graduate studies. Several months passed and June arrived. Father's Day was fast approaching. I decided to attend church that Sunday and joined in singing songs of praise. Everyone asked how I was doing, and I answered, "Fine." Well, I thought I was fine, but suddenly as I bowed my head to pray at the very end of the service, I passed out cold.

When I came back to consciousness, I was laid out flat on the table in the church library. An ear, nose, and throat doctor was hovering over me, slapping my face and trying to get me to wake up. I did not know what had happened or where I was. I did realize my hands were all curled up rigidly and tightly against my body. The doctor said I had just experienced a grand mal seizure and was being transported to the local hospital for emergency treatment. What a day that was!

In the emergency room, I was given an IV to keep me safe. After the doctor evaluated me, he said I should not be alone. Wait a minute—I was alone. Now what would I do? A friend from church had followed the ambulance to the hospital and offered to let me stay with her and her husband until I was well enough to stay by myself. So I stayed with this university couple, with my little doggie, until I was well enough to stay by myself. In the meantime, another friend drove me to a neurologist to have my brain evaluated. Much to my amazement, my brain waves were abnormal. I was placed on heavy medication to stop any more seizures. When I took the medication, however, it made me sleep all day long.

At this point, our youngest daughter came home to live with me after her worldwide tour with the Up with People organization. Because of my medical condition, I was temporarily dropped from my teaching and graduate studies. After several months, I continued graduate school and completed my education.

Feeling much better, I found a group meeting at the local church called "Single, Single Again." I decided to attend and move on from the seizure event. Several people attended—some single by choice and others single due to the death of a spouse. They met every week at the church and offered amazing programs, such as hiking, cooking, and relationship skills.

I really enjoyed the group and settled in as a consistent member of the club. They even had a fun gathering after the meeting called After Glow—a meeting at a local restaurant to fellowship and have some fun food to end the evening. The group was very supportive about the loss of my husband, and the programs were very stimulating as well as fun.

Starting life over was a new beginning for me, as I had been with my husband since I was 15 years old. Now I had to begin a new chapter of life. Graduate school was a challenge, and I loved the teaching opportunity offered to me. I began to spread my life out and not focus constantly on the past pain. From day one, I always listened for God's voice for direction in my life, and now was no different. I would get quiet, pray to my Heavenly Father, and wait for directions from the Holy Spirit.

12

Pain and Healing

Life was going on and pulling me along with it. I was in a tailspin of events—rushing from here to there, spending time in the library, and attending graduate classes. Yes, I was busy, but I always took time to process my grief. Allowing yourself to feel sad and cry is a very important part of healing. Tears are really liquid love for the person who has left your life. When you are a confessed follower of Christ, you know that one day, you will be together again in heaven. Granted, there is no marriage in heaven, but you will still be with other loved ones. Following Christ means having a strong commitment to staying in God's will, reading the Bible, and learning His commandments so you can live your faith out in front of others. God has a purpose and a plan for our lives, as stated in Jeremiah. 29:11: "'For I know the plans I have for you' declares the Lord, 'plans to prosper you and not to harm you, plans to give you hope and a future.'" I decided to really lean on the Lord during this painful time of loneliness.

> *Trust in the Lord with all your heart and do not lean on your own understanding.*
> *—Proverbs 3:5-6*

I made a new commitment to pray every single day for our daughters, family, friends, and even my enemies. I prayed that our daughters would love deeply, sincerely, and sacrificially—seeing and loving others as God loves. I prayed that I would be empowered to daily model God's love and compassion for our daughters and others in my life. I prayed that our daughters would pray every single day of their lives.

In 1 John 5:14, God promises us that "this is the confidence that we have toward him, that if we ask anything according to his will, he hears us" (1 John 5:14). When I joined the church, I was given a life verse from the Bible, which I attempted to live out every day: "Let your light so shine before others, that they may see your good works and give glory to God who is in Heaven" (Matt. 5:16)!

As the days and weeks passed, the pain subsided a little in my broken heart. I began to pray for God to clearly show me His will for my life. I prayed, "God, bless me in my singleness. I really don't want to go out on a date at the age of 40; however, if it is your will, I will obey." I told God, "I need a man who loves you deeply, Lord. I need a man who has no exes in Texas. I need a man who does not want any children—I am just way too old to start over with girls in college. Oh, God, please let this new man live on a farm, as growing up on a farm was a dream come true. So, God, if your will is for me to get remarried, then please hear my prayers."

The weeks turned into months and the months turned into years, which flew past. Then a man in the Single, Single Again group, asked me out on a movie date. I was very cautious about the request, as I was still grieving, but I wanted to move on with my life.

I said yes to the movie date, and it went well. I asked him many questions, and guess what? He had never been married before. He did not want any children. He lived on his grandparents' farm, and most importantly, he loved his Lord and Savior. Wow, we had a lot in common, and he wanted me to come out to the farm for a visit.

Was I curious? Sure, but very cautious in going forward with the friendship. I saw him weekly at the meetings at church and enjoyed his company very much. I eventually met his family on a holiday. His father was deceased, but his mother was a precious little old lady—full of laughter and joy. His two older sisters were married with children.

I was very attracted to this man's love for his Lord and Savior. He always led the Single, Single Again meetings and opened each meeting with prayer. As my heart healed and my graduate studies went well, we continued to date and spend time on his farm. One Sunday, he attended my church service and we made friends with other couples. My heart was healing!

13

Life Goes Forward

The same Sunday that my friend visited my church service, we sat right next to a young couple our age. They told us their last name was Duran. *Wow*, that was the same surname as my new friend. Was that a surprise or what? So it was not a random meeting. We became fast friends and had a lot in common.

The wife was from Holland, so she was away from family and friends and latched on to me as a mentor quickly. She was expecting her first child, and we were all excited together! One day the phone rang, and the husband was in a panic, telling us that his wife had gone into premature labor. I rode in the ambulance with her on the way to the hospital, and my friend drove the anxious father to the hospital. The baby was delivered safely by C-section and placed in ICU for observation. I stayed in the room with the mother, and the two men watched over the baby boy in the nursery. By the end of the day, all was settled and we went back home. The next week the mother and baby boy were able to come home as well. Everything seemed to be just fine.

As time went on, my friend and I spent more and more time together—on walks, hikes, and other dates with our new friends. We often had meals together and enjoyed movies as well. Our friendship was growing. I was about to graduate from college and secure a new job. The graduation ceremony was scheduled, and my entire family attended the big event. I was awarded my hard-earned diploma, and then we all went out to celebrate my success by going out to an amazing dining place nearby.

After graduation, I was hired as an intake counselor for the local Job Corps program. This was an excellent fit for me, as I was versed in the communication program and had always worked with students. I met with the students as they entered the program of study. Each student was offered an education plus career training, such as for nurse's aide and computer skills. Housing was available for over 1,200 students coming from all parts of the country, mostly Oklahoma and Texas. Many students graduated with an education and a life skill. What an amazing job for a communications major who loved to talk. The days were long, and the work was enjoyable. I made many new friends.

The job eventually got easier, and the students were a wonderful part of the program. I taught them social skills and how to deal with personal and on-the-job conflicts. The emphasis of the program was for at-risk students who needed to complete their high school education and learn a new skill to provide a living for themselves. Hundreds of at-risk students attended the program, and they proved successful in their endeavors—graduating with working skills. Many students graduated with training so they could secure jobs and live a life of productivity. Many registered nurse's aides, auto repairmen, and computer-skilled graduates went out into the working world.

At this same time, my friend was a certified respiratory

therapist, working at a hospital while living on his grand-father's farm. He drove into town to attend the Single, Single Again meetings. Then he returned to the farm to go to work every day.

Our relationship continued to blossom and bloom into a full-blown love affair. We discussed getting married at some point, but not real soon. My heart still ached at times, so we moved forward slowly. One night, I surprised my parents for their anniversary. I rented a limousine, and we took them to a very special dining area.

After the evening ended, my friend asked my dad for his permission to marry me. He answered, "Yes, of course." My friend got down on his knees and asked for my hand in marriage. We set the date for the next year in March at our local church. My sisters and daughters were my brides-maids, and my husband-to-be asked his close friend to be his best man. All was set, and now my healing was com-plete. Life was again filled with love, joy, happiness, peace, and honesty. We planned to spend our honeymoon in the Pocono Mountains.

14

The Wedding

The invitations were in the mail, and the date was set. The church was reserved, and the ministers were willing to perform the ceremony. The rings were purchased, and the wedding party was cemented.

I had selected my wedding dress, the bridesmaids had tried on their dresses, and the men's tuxedos were all ordered. A coworker made the wedding cake, and the food for the reception was ordered. To my surprise, many of my friends and family were traveling from Ohio to attend the wedding.

Even my elderly godmother was flying into the Texas airport to add to the wedding joy and blessing. And my long-time 4-H friend attended to clog to her favorite song at the reception. What an exciting time! After all the sadness and brokenness, it was time to celebrate life.

The day finally arrived, and the church was packed with family, friends, neighbors, and coworkers. The organ began to play, and my goddaughter flew in from Ohio and sang a beautiful solo. Then we repeated our vows in front of my big brother, who is a minister. The ceremony ended with many smiles and hugs, and then we went into the reception hall to complete the celebration. The food was excellent, and then my friend clogged to an Elvis Presley recording.

The best man read a reading in the couple's honor, and my big brother led us in an opening prayer before we enjoyed the banquet. I surprised everyone and sang "Stand by Your Man" by Tammy Wynette. The entire assembly gasped as I grabbed the microphone and blasted out the song.

Then came the cutting of the cake, and of course, the groom had to put the cake up the bride's nose, smearing the frosting all over my face. What fun everyone had! Next came the tossing of the garter to the next man to get engaged and married. Then the reception ended, and everyone left to fly back home. It was an amazing celebration of love and joy!

Now it was time for the honeymoon. After the reception, we drove to Austin to catch an airplane to the Pocono Resort in Scranton, Pennsylvania. We had reservations to spend the week at the resort. The honeymoon suite had three floors. The bottom floor was a heart-shaped pool and sauna. The top floor was a heart-shaped bed surrounded by mirrors. The other room was a complete bathroom overlooking a living room with a large fireplace. The upstairs bathroom housed a champagne glass hot tub.

We could pick up the telephone and call the love machine. The van picked us up and took us anywhere we wanted to go—to the ice skating rink, the basketball court, or to the main lodge where they served amazing meals. We were entertained by the one and only Howie Mandell. He was very funny to everyone in the audience. The next day, we went snowmobiling in the woods on campus. Later that night, we played a game of "Name That Tune," and my new husband won the big award by naming each tune played. I was just beside myself with pride!

Back in our honeymoon suite, we loved to sit in the hot sauna and relax, and then slip into the swimming pool and enjoy the fireplace before going to bed. The heart-shaped bed was very comfortable, as well as my new husband's strong, hot body. We made love and slipped off to sleep, being very exhausted. Night after night, we had great meals, excellent entertainment, and fun bowling.

One day we went cross-country skiing and had a blast in the snow. Since my new husband had grown up in south Texas, he had never been in the snow before. On the other hand, I had grown up in Northern Ohio and spent every winter in the snow belt. One day we even went to a shooting range, and my husband taught me some sharpshooting tips. He had spent many years with his father on hunting trips to kill deer and bring them home to process and enjoy for months to come. The honeymoon holds many memories for us.

15

Coming Back to *Real* Life

After the honeymoon was over, it was back to the farm and our daily grind at our job sites. The first thing we did together was build the emu pens out of chain-link material. I knew how to run the tractor, so I dug the fence posts. We then decided to purchase some emus to raise on the farm. We had three pairs that we named Ricky and Lucy and Bill and Hillary. They were amazing birds, like nothing either of us had before in our lifetime. The other pair of birds we named after my parents, Howard and Lee. All the birds did very well laying eggs, and the males did the incubation job of sitting on the nest of eggs.

The birds themselves were very delightful and almost majestic! The feathers were used for fashion, and the gallons of oil on their backs were very absorbable for all uses such as sports strains or arthritis pain. The leather was needed to make boots, belts, and purses. Even the very hard and dark green eggs were made into small purses.

After many months, we joined the National Emu Association. However, the American Beef Association was very powerful in Texas, and the emu association didn't get off the ground. We lost all our money and ended up giving the emus away to local farmers, as we didn't have the market to sell them. That was a sad, sad day.

Later we tried market goats, but we were hit by a long, serious drought and had to get rid of them. Then I said, "Let's raise chocolate Labrador retrievers." Since President Clinton had one in the White House, the breed was very popular. I went out and purchased five females—three chocolate and two black—and one happy daddy dog. The first year was a waiting game until they were 12 months old, and then the puppies started to appear—just in time for Christmas. All the puppies were sold in a matter of days as people came from Austin to buy them.

That was a fun year with both of us on our jobs and still celebrating our honeymoon of new love, surrounded by puppies.

Godiva Gale Bosco

The farm was green with grass, and the cows loved the water tanks on the farm to cool off in the hot summer heat.

At work one day, I got a call from an old rancher friend who wanted me to buy her 15 donkeys. The donkeys were in high demand for area ranchers to protect the baby calves as the donkeys fought off the coyotes and saved the calves from death. This saved the ranchers much-needed cash for each calf they could sell at auction.

When we were headed down the interstate with our truck and trailer full of donkeys, my husband said, "We are hauling *ass* now"! He is a very funny man!

We were very happy in our new home with all the animals, cows, donkeys, and dogs. Life had been a tremendous fumble in the past, but now God was at work in our lives to renew our hope. Things were looking up, and we had completely remodeled the 100-year-old farmhouse with a brand-new kitchen and new air conditioner, which the old house had never had before.

As the years rolled past, my mother-in-law told me an amazing secret about my new husband. After their two daughters were born, her husband insisted she get her fallopian tubes cut. She obeyed her husband's wishes. Fifteen years later, her doctor said she was pregnant with her third child. The fallopian tubes had grown back together, and she gave birth to my husband.

What a miracle. What a sovereign God we serve, to take my first husband home in a flash and then make me move to Texas to marry a new, amazing Christian man who didn't want any children. It is almost too much to believe that our God is so loving that He loves us just where we are, and as broken sinners, we are welcomed into the family of God! I am here to encourage everyone reading this book to put their full trust in Christ Jesus as your Lord and Savior. He is love, grace, peace, kindness, patience, and joy—all the fruit of the Spirit.

16

Death by Hanging

The days, weeks, and months were flying by, and my oldest daughter fell in love with a blind man at the School for the Blind in Columbus, Ohio. He was an awesome person and had a ton of courage. He was born blind and was always discriminated against because of his unusual eye movements. Life was more than challenging for him. He had a painful childhood, as many made fun of him.

He and my daughter dated for years and then decided to get married. Afterward, they moved to Texas. He eventually got hired in a federal building to manage a food court. He was very good at his job as manager, and things were looking good. In the meantime, our daughter was working at Dallas Children's Hospital as a registered nurse, specializing in heart transplants. As the years rolled by, our son-in-law was an amazing husband and even attended a spiritual weekend event.

The world we live in is constantly pulling us down into phases of self-pity and guilt. Everyone faces decisions daily—what to think, what to say, and how to react to others. The Bible tells us, "As a man thinketh so he is" (Prov. 23:7). Our thoughts are so very powerful that we need to capture each and every thought.

The power of the world is many times more inviting than following God's way. Satan pulls us down in every moment of the day. He wants to destroy our lives and confuse us with all his lies. We need to know what the Scripture tells us so we can pray before each decision and honor God in everything we do.

Dallas is not unlike any other large metro city—drugs abound everywhere. Many drug dealers are willing to sell you opiates to ruin your life. They don't consider your life—only the money they can steal from you to get you hooked and addicted, because that means steady income for them.

Our new son-in-law was being hunted down by a local drug dealer, being pulled into the addictive drugs he was selling. Now, we all know that drugs can take over our minds, allowing us to make bad choices and bringing our entire world down on top of us.

Just like alcohol, drugs can ruin your life, your job, your family, and your entire world is under attack when the addictive behaviors begin to take over your life. It is always tempting to remain in a haze of alcohol and drugs when your life has unmanageable pain and misery is pounding down on your heart day after day. We are all broken sinners, and yet God continues to call our names and offer hope. His love is much more powerful than drugs and alcohol; however, as broken people, we look for the easy way out of misery.

Our son-in-law became consumed by illegal drugs so that he could not think rationally. His wife, his father-in-law, and his entire family loved him so very much and were asking God Almighty to save his life and take away the addiction to the drugs ruining his life. We need to acknowledge the fact that drugs are stealing our husbands, children, and grandchildren.

What can we as a family do to protect our loved ones?

We can inform ourselves to understand the amazing power that drugs can have on our minds. We can speak up and encourage public officials to clamp down on local drug dealers and make the offense more punishable by law. We can offer more public workshops to educate families and individuals about how to get help if their loved one gets involved with drugs. There are many helpful programs in our cities that can turn the addictive behaviors around and help the person return to a healthy lifestyle.

We need to attack this opiate epidemic with all forces, on all sides—with families as well as lawmakers. The more we are educated about the destructive power drugs can have on our society, the better opportunity we have to defeat the epidemic itself. We need to stand up and protect our families from all the dangers around us.

Unfortunately, one day our daughter came home from her job at the Dallas Children's hospital and found the house empty, or so she thought. When she noticed that the dogs were outside on the deck, she was very confused about why they weren't in the house as usual. She wondered where her husband was and was very concerned. She opened the garage door to go out and do some laundry … CRASH … CRASH … CRASH …

There in front of her was her beloved husband hanging from the garage ceiling. *This isn't really happening!* she said to herself.

Even though she had supported her husband time after time after time throughout different rehab programs, he was addicted to drugs. She had always believed that her husband could beat the addiction, and she never gave up on his fighting spirit. However, in front of her eyes was her worse fear ever. He had hung himself and was already dead too long to even try to revive him. She rushed to the phone to call 911.

The police quickly arrived and came to her assistance. The rest of the day was a haze as she remained in shock for the rest of the week, unwilling to believe that her husband was really dead. How could this be? Over and over the horror went through her mind.

This was a horrible nightmare crashing down around her. What steps would she take now? What options did she have?

Friends and family were contacted, and the funeral was packed—not an empty seat was available. The pastor conducted the service, and her husband's body was cremated. The weeks dragged on and on. Our daughter was very distraught yet allowed her deep, abiding faith in her Lord and Savior to carry her through. Life would go on with or without her husband. She returned to her nursing position at the hospital and pushed forward.

Our daughter was in great pain. When we are in pain, God's love pours all over us. God hurts when we hurt. All good fathers realize pain is a part of the process of moving past death. Life is very sacred—it is a gift. It should never be taken for granted. Life can be snatched away in a breathless moment. Life is designed to prepare us and shape us for eternity.

Remember, when we struggle through death and loss, we learn struggle is a *gift*! Think about it—small investments end up as big dividends.

After many months, my daughter became friends with a young man in her unit. He was from New Orleans and was looking for a good Christian woman to marry.

Our daughter realized her Lord and Savior was

answering all her prayers to put a new man in her life forever and ever.

17

Starting Over

After several years, our daughter was deeply in love with her new man. They got engaged and set a date to get married in New Orleans, Louisiana. We gathered in the large church with family, friends, and loved ones filling the church to overflowing. The bridesmaids were in full attire, as were the groomsmen. The organ played the wedding march, and the ceremony began with the bride on her dad's arm floating down the aisle like an angel—dressed in a beautiful gown of lace and a flowing headpiece to match. The bridesmaids were in their places facing the congregation and supporting the bride and groom. The bride's sister was her maid of honor. The bride and groom repeated their vows to each other.

The ceremony ended, and the church emptied to travel over to a beautiful banquet hall where the reception took place. With a band swinging to the beat of the music and everyone out on the dance floor, the celebration had begun. Many pictures were taken of the wedding party and the family. Everyone celebrated with the newlyweds, and when the party was over, everyone went home. The newlyweds left on their honeymoon to New Orleans and would return to the Dallas area to continue their new lives working at the Children's hospital together.

Their firstborn was a tiny baby girl weighing in at six pounds. She lit up their lives and added to their joy. The next child to arrive was a bouncing baby boy. He joined the family to make it a foursome. While working at the Dallas Children's hospital, the couple was very busy raising their new children and moving into a new home with a swimming pool. Then several years later, the third child entered the family scene—another baby girl weighing in at seven pounds. Each child was baptized at six weeks in the local church, being raised in the Christian faith. Each child had a set of godparents to hold them accountable to their faith and help them follow Jesus through their entire lifetime.

Soon the couple welcomed other children into their lives and become foster parents for unwanted children in the Dallas area. They welcomed many children over the next few years, offering them unconditional love and affection. Many came with abuse issues and needed to be adopted treated with special acceptance.

Over several years, they decide to adopt one of the infants in their care. The mother was a prostitute in the streets of Dallas, and this the fourth baby she had dropped off at the hospital. The baby was delivered to the couple's home when he was two days old, and they promised to love him. He was surrounded by love, as at this time there were other children, and the baby was held, rocked, and smothered with love.

The little boy never spoke a single word during his life because the mother had done drugs during her pregnancy. Years later, they adopted a teenager; however, when he turned 18, he ran away from the family's discipline, not wanting to take responsibility for his actions. This goes to show you that all children need to be brought up in the love of Christ. If they are taught at a young age, they will not depart from it. This young man was not taught about the Love of Christ, and he has been pulled into the depths of the world's wicked culture. Seeing the young man get into trouble and leave their loving home after he was adopted broke the mother and father's heart.

This reminds me of James 5:13,16: "Is anyone in trouble? He should pray .... The prayer of a righteous man is powerful and effective."

When you are a foster home you need endurance, the power to hold on to your faith and keep believing in the promise God has for your life. Families also need encouragement, fresh courage to square their shoulders and move forward in faith. The Bible tells us in Proverbs 3:5, *Lean on the Lord and not your own understanding.* When we lean on the Lord, we find *hope.* This is a settled confidence that the God who loves us will work night and day on our behalf as we place our trust in Him.

Losing their newly adopted son was a hard time for our family—it was very painful. Pain has a way of overriding everything we know to be right and moral. When we are in pain, we need someone there to hold our hand, wipe our tears away, or simply to stand by our side.

18

Another Wedding

With two daughters in our lives, we were very excited when daughter number two announced her engagement, and the wedding date was set to take place in the Texas Hill Country. The wedding was set, and many family and friends came from Ohio to support the new couple with prayers and hugs. The wedding was held outdoors, and the weather was absolutely beautiful. The vows were exchanged, and the reception began with a bridal party dance. The couple departed, headed to their honeymoon, and came back to resume their jobs in Austin.

Daughter number two was diagnosed with bipolar disorder and was placed on strong medication. However, with her father being an alcoholic, she soon found herself ravaged by drinking, drowning her troubles in a gray haze. At one point, her husband reached out to ask for help in dealing with her drinking, but no one reached deep down into their heart to give her help.

One day I called my daughter on the phone, and when she answered, I could hear slurred speech and suddenly lost connection with her as the phone went dead. I quickly called 911 and had them break into the house, where our daughter was found unconscious on the couch. The emergency squad transported her to the local hospital, where they pumped her stomach, as she had taken many pills and washed them down with liquor. She survived and returned home.

Afterward, her marriage quickly dissolved, with her husband regularly verbally abusing her, causing her to attempt suicide. The abuse was nothing new, as her husband was very nasty to her in and out of the relationship. They visited a counselor for new communication patterns but to no avail. The husband was diagnosed with narcissistic personality disorder and was not willing to get any counseling to help him improve his lifestyle. After years of counseling, the marriage ended in divorce, which saved our daughter's life.

Was our daughter in pain? The pain was searing through our entire family. God hates divorce—it is a form of death. Death, grief, and loss is a process. Do not be afraid to fail. If we never fail, we will not need a God or Savior. Because of fear, we have access to *grace*. We need to push through death to experience the euphoria and ecstasy of grace. The psalmist writes:

> Lord, if you kept a record of our sins,
>> Who, O Lord could ever survive?
> But, you offer forgiveness,
>> That we might learn to fear you
> I am counting on the Lord;
> I am counting on the Lord;
>> yes, I am counting on him.
>> I have put my hope in his word. (Ps. 130:3-5)

19

A Brand-New Life

Life after alcohol abuse was not easy, but our daughter threw her faith into the helpful group called Alcoholics Anonymous. It's a self-help group for people fighting the ravage of alcohol in their lives. Their policy is "Let go and let God."

Of course, this was not a simple fix, and our daughter dug deep into her faith to change her lifestyle and become sober. Today, she is sober and is leading a group to walk alongside them and encourage them to stay sober! Her leadership style is like no other as she reminds them *to let go and let God!* Our daughter was influenced in her faith by her entire family, including her grandparents and parents. *She was raised in the Christian faith and as she grew older, she did not depart from it (Prov. 22:6).*

Today, she is strong, sober, and focused on her life going forward. From the depths of alcoholism, she fought her way out with God by her side and the help of others encouraging her.

In the AA organization, you are assigned a sponsor who can walk alongside you through thick and thin, encouraging you to stay sober and lean on their leadership. The group follows a 12-step program and uses the Serenity

Prayer at every meeting:

> God grant me the Serenity
> to accept the things
> I cannot change;
> Courage to change the things I can;
> and Wisdom to know the difference.

For many people in desperate situations, seeking peace, strength, and wisdom, these simple words, whispered to God as they understand Him, have seen them through their darkest hours. They have come to believe that the prayer can connect them with the God of their higher power, helping them face their addictions.

My daughter spent more time in prayer and seeking God's will for her new life. She began performing acts of kindness repeatedly in her new community. She loved serving the needs of those around her. She began to embrace and celebrate serving others, and it brightened her life. She was no longer self-centered, and the grief and sorrow of the divorce left her heart. She did not let the sorrow of divorce get blown out of proportion but allowed herself to cry, grieve, and heal.

20

Listening to God's Voice

Years went by, and my new husband and I had completely remodeled the 100-year-old farmhouse where we began our new married lives.

One morning, my husband sat up in bed and announced, "We are moving up to Dallas to help raise the grandchildren with a biblical base!"

I responded, "Oh Really!"

That's all it took to move to Dallas into a little rented house. My husband was offered a $10,000 bonus to sign on with Cook Children's Hospital in Fort Worth, Texas. My husband was overwhelmed by his decision to move to the Dallas area.

Wow, when God opens a door, and you are listening to His voice, He will guide you in the best direction and always reward your obedience. Now, what would I do with my time and talent? When we got settled into our new house, I looked across the interstate highway and what did I see? A brand-new community college offering a position to teach in my master's degree major: *communications!* This was unbelievable; I loved teaching students.

I started with the fall semester and taught four different sections to start my new career. What a blessing when God opens a door, you can walk right into a perfect opportunity sponsored by God himself. For the next 10 years, I served in this college and received a monthly teacher's retirement benefit! What an amazing gift from God!

For the next 10 years, I drove across the street and taught my classes in the community college. I loved teaching and being with the students. Everywhere we went, I ran into a student who said hello to me. What a true blessing. One semester, we were studying persuasive communication skills and I got guest speakers to come and present how they conquered their drug addiction at a local Christian treatment center.

Then the students had to write an essay on the impact the speaker had upon their values. Almost all 75 students enjoyed the presentation, except for one. This student said to me, "You cannot bring those Bible Bangers into the classroom." Well, I was not allowed to continue teaching after that class, so that was the end of my teaching career. I enjoyed teaching, and with the drug culture of today, I would do the same exact presentation all over again—even if it's just to help one student.

You may wonder what happened to the farmhouse. Well, God had that in His hands as well. A retired couple from Houston had a horse and wanted to rent the farmhouse. They moved in and took excellent care of the homestead for years, enjoying watching the cattle on the back acreage and having their horse in the pasture field. They enjoyed the country living and not having any chores to perform. They were delightful and took excellent care of our little farmhouse.

A perfect plan for both couples!

21

Grandchildren Are a Gift

Proverbs 17:6 tells us, "Grandchildren are the crown of the aged."

Now our family life is very close-knit, and we talk to one another almost daily. Many families are spread out all over the United States; however, families are forever. Being a grandparent is meant to be a blessing. It is an honor to have raised a child who brings forth another generation of children and to have lived long enough to witness it. With this blessing comes a responsibility. "A good man leaves an inheritance to his children's children (Prov. 13:22)—a heritage of faith. Grandparents have a responsibility to share with their grandchildren their knowledge of God and bear witness to what He has done in their lives.

My husband and I have many God stories to share with our grandchildren. It is a blessing and responsibility to minister to the children when they are young, to build a biblical base for them to live by. Our culture is wicked and pulling our children in the wrong direction. Good morals are a basic building block for all children to know as they leave home and face the wicked world.

God designed the grandchild/grandparent relationship to be a reciprocal one of love and care—flowing from each side to meet the physical, emotional, and spiritual needs of each person. God has given us His Word that we might learn to live out His beautiful design.

Our first granddaughter came in at 6 pounds and 10 ounces. She grew up to be a beautiful young lady whose parents taught her the Word and Christian values. She graduated from high school and then attended Texas A&M college. Then came our first grandson, coming in at seven pounds. He graduated from high school with honors and earned a full scholarship to Southern Mississippi College in Hattiesburg Mississippi.

The next grandchild came along at seven pounds, four ounces and was a spitfire—with a fierce focus on making sure her dreams were achieved. She is still in high school as this is being written; however, she has her sights set on attending Louisiana State University. The fourth child arrived at two days old as a foster baby from the Fort Worth area. As previously stated, his mother was a homeless, drug-addicted prostitute who had abandoned him at the hospital.

The fifth child arrived at age 16 as another foster child. At age 17, he was adopted into the family. His father was dead, and his mother was in prison. He did not get a biblical foundation in his teen years, and when he turned 18, he dropped out of high school and ran away. He touches base with us occasionally but is still not settled into our family unit. He has jumped from job to job.

I hope you can all sense the importance of bringing up a child with a biblical foundation. When the child is left to themselves, they will fall into temptation and into Satan's traps over and over.

I hope by reading this book, you have gathered some wisdom about how families need to be loved unconditionally—the same way God loves us. We need to humble ourselves and be obedient to God's Word. The Word is a very powerful two-edged sword that can cut through poisonous lies, deception, and Satanic tricks that can pull us into addictions. We can lose our lives when we fall into sinful lifestyles.

Pay close attention to how you raise your children and grandchildren. Our culture is out to trip up our youth by feeding them lies and covering up the truth. If Satan can take down the *family*, he can take down the entire *nation*! Wake up and take responsibility for raising your children and grandchildren. It is all about the future of our nation. Lean on the Lord!

22

Let Your Light So Shine

I was so taken aback by the adoption of my grandson who was the product of a prostitute that I decided to write a book about him.

The morning after I prayed about it, I woke up with the title in my mind—*One Million Babies*. I knew out of one million babies, this baby changed the fabric of our family unit.

The mother had already abandoned three other babies at the local Dallas hospital. All of them were in institutions and could not speak, due to the mother's drug use. The mother did not know who the father of her child was, but the baby was very handsome. As time went on, the foster child captured the family's hearts, and we decided to adopt him. So I was excited to author my book about the little abandoned baby boy now entering our family.

I eventually completed the first draft of the book. Now how would I publish it? I prayed, and that same day, my brother called from South Carolina. I told my brother about publishing the book, and he happened to know a book publisher who was a strong Christian and had just graduated with his degree in publishing. The young man was the son of my brother's good friend. What an answer to a prayer!

I called the publisher that afternoon to make arrangements to send him my rough draft copy. He happened to live in Texas, as I did. Things went forward quickly, and the publisher offered me a good discount on his professional work and getting my book onto Amazon.

I worked very steadily on the book, and finally, it was ready to publish after many corrections and prayerful considerations. As I was a former foster parent myself, I included a workbook about the steps needed to become a foster home. I was raised in a Christian home, so I was very pro-life in my moral beliefs. I knew I could let my light shine, telling others that adoption was the best option. I was strongly committed to influencing others to save all innocent babies from the horrible death of abortion.

I dedicated my time in my community to all programs that invited me to talk about pro-life and family. I truly believe it is God's will for all children to be gifted with a strong, loving home that raised the child with godly morals and faith.

I speak in my community as well as in several areas throughout Texas. I committed to the program 40 Days of Life. I stood in front of the local planned parenthood organization for 40 days. Many of my friends stood out by the interstate and held up signs reading: "Pray to Stop Abortion." Many bystanders harassed us and yelled obscenities as they drove past. All of my friends stood strong and prayed for the unborn babies as we worked for the 40 Days of Life. As a result, one planned parenthood program closed its doors!

Now the book was almost complete, and I gave the rough draft to my publisher. It did not take too long before I selected a design for the cover and created the back cover with my deep conviction about how the book could encourage a woman to put her child up for adoption and not choose abortion.

I also volunteered in a local store named Twice As Nice. All local folks donated very lightly used items and new items to resell. The money went to the girls who chose to keep their babies. The store not only offered counseling but formula, diapers, clothing, and furniture for the child. The store was very successful and supported the mothers who raised their child instead of choosing abortion.

My book was published and sold very well on Amazon—getting many positive reviews from readers. I gave the profits from the book sales to my grandson's family because he needed many special therapies at home and at school. He was very successful at school. Like God had impacted my thoughts, the little boy certainly affected the family in a bold, loving manner. His brothers and sisters were very protective and loving to the little guy. He was labeled autistic; however, he was very lovable, cuddly, and silly. He loved being around people and learning how to use his iPad to communicate his wants.

The boy has just turned 13 as this book is being written, and he is the center of attention in our little family. He loves going to Sunday School and church. He is very helpful around the house. He gets himself dressed and walks out to the school bus when it stops in front of the house to take him to school every day. He is certainly "One in a Million," and he has impacted our entire world in an amazing way. We thank God every day for placing him in our family and in our lives!

Since we only have today to love the little guy, we lean on the Lord's guidance for his future, knowing it's in His hands. If you ask his sister if she will allow him to be put into an institution, she will tell you, "No Way"! He will live with my husband and me forever. Now that is *love*, as she is only 17 years old and does not see marriage in her future for several years! This little boy is surely "One in a Million"! All children need unconditional love the same way our Heavenly Father loves us, with grace and kindness.

We are to live the words of the Bible and *"love one another"*!

23

Stand Strong

After 20 years of marriage, my husband suffered from intense pain in his groin area. Our local family doctor couldn't give a successful diagnosis, so we traveled back and forth to Downtown Dallas to see a specialist. This went on for a year without relief. Each doctor tried a different treatment. After three years, my husband took short-term disability from his hospital job as a respiratory therapist. The pain was so intense he didn't get much sleep, and this continued night after night.

Finally, a local doctor suggested surgery to clip the nerves in his groin area. During the follow-up appointment, the surgeon was astonished that the clipping of the nerves did not provide any relief whatsoever. Time dragged on and we continued to deal with the horrible pain and misery. One doctor gave my husband a prescription for Oxycodone. Over time, my husband became addicted to it.

I never saw my husband so depressed. He would cry, shake, and was in horrible pain with no relief. Then one morning, he said, "Take the guns out of the house. I am considering shooting myself to end my misery!" I quickly went into action and removed the guns and called the local Behavioral Center of Health. I got him admitted to the clinic, and he stayed for two weeks. Then I brought him home and things improved.

The only way to make it through this struggle was by reaching out to other Christians and praying every single day for the strength to continue. After several months, the clipping of the nerve ending healed and relieved my husband of his pain. What a miracle!

He went back to work at the hospital, only to face the COVID-19 epidemic. My husband was very weak and not capable of going back to work on a full-time schedule. He tried to go back, but the 12 hours shifts were just too much for him to deal with.

He treated COVID-19 patients all day long, and it was very stressful. So he requested a different schedule and started working three days a week. He made it through the day dealing with all the emergencies, but several of his coworkers were hospitalized with the disease. Well, things get worse.

Under the stress of the COVID-19 epidemic and the lockdown, things increasingly declined. As a married couple, we sleep in separate rooms and continue to clean the entire house over and over, sanitizing all surfaces. We knew that the virus lived for three days on the surfaces of our home and all over the vehicles.

Sleep was a stressful event. With my husband being on short-term disability, I ended my retirement and got a job at the local hospital screening visitors and employees for COVID-19. I wore a mask and worked seven days a week to help our finances. Both my husband and I leaned on the Lord during these months.

We attempted to continue our weekly Bible study series online via Zoom. Many people were stressed about doing the study online for security reasons. I, on the other hand, had a group called "Grace Girls," and we usually met monthly to study the book of Philippians. Now with the epidemic smothering groups and travel, this group also struggled to meet in person.

Yes, we miss one another; however, God pulls us closer in times of trials. Over and over in my life, God has pulled me through struggles over difficult times and blessed my life richly. God promises never to leave us, and you can count on God—He will never ever leave you!

We all have struggles to face. Life is about overcoming broken lives that are being pulled toward sin by Satan. Facing death, painful events, and the illness of loved ones is *life*. Starting over in a new day!

I want to leave you with some tips for working your way through grief, death, and disappointments in your lifetime. The following are just a few ideas for how you can manage your pain and loss.

#1. Light Up

Remember, even though your light is dim, you can practice my favorite Bible verse, Matthew 5:16, "Let your light so shine before all men, that they may see your good works and give glory to your father who is in heaven."

#2. Dress Up

Do not allow yourself to get sloppy. Stay in great health, fix your hair, and have fun walking for exercise.

#3. Stand Up

Each day is a new day, and you can assume the best time of your life is just beginning. Trust that your Savior will open new doors for you, and know that God has a loving plan for your life!

#4. Start Up

Every morning is a good time to start a new habit. You can begin with prayer, praise, and song. You will notice an improvement in your morning, and it will continue into your day!

#5. Shut Up

Many times, you may find yourself in a pity party over your sadness in loss and death. Well, guess what—tell the devil to shut up, do not believe his lies, and kick despair to the curb!

#6. Look Up

If you find yourself depending on no one except "*you*," look up to God who made you so very special. He can offer you hope and healing and give you a new heart, a new beginning.

Go ahead, ask God for courage and you will be filled with hope not just because you serve the Lord, but because God hears all of our prayers.

In Ephesians 5:22, God tells us to choose the Lord every morning.

Now, when you do all these steps and still have bad days, remember God promises never to leave you. So I pray you will be able to change your sorrow and sadness into joy and gladness!

Wait and see—your tears of sadness are really just

liquid love for the people and things you have lost. Take baby steps to recover into a brand-new life, leaning on the Lord. You just may find yourself repeating these steps over and over and creating a new lifestyle for yourself. Be kind to yourself and always remember, God has your back!

Made in the USA
Columbia, SC
30 May 2021